Bluetick Coonhounds

Paige V. Polinsky

Checkerboard
Library

An Imprint of Abdo Publishing
abdopublishing.com

abdopublishing.com

Published by Abdo Publishing, a division of ABDO, PO Box 398166, Minneapolis, MN 55439. Copyright © 2017 by Abdo Consulting Group, Inc. International copyrights reserved in all countries. No part of this book may be reproduced in any form without written permission from the publisher. Checkerboard Library™ is a trademark and logo of Abdo Publishing.

Printed in the United States of America, North Mankato, Minnesota.
062016
092016

Cover Photo: iStockphoto
Interior Photos: Animal Photography, p. 7; AP Images, p. 9; iStockphoto, pp. 11, 17; Shutterstock, pp. 1, 13, 19; SuperStock, pp. 5, 15; Zachary Boumeester, p. 21

Series Coordinator: Tamara L. Britton
Editor: Liz Salzmann
Production: Mighty Media, Inc.

Library of Congress Cataloging-in-Publication Data

Names: Polinsky, Paige V., author.
Title: Bluetick coonhounds / Paige V. Polinsky.
Description: Minneapolis, MN : Abdo Publishing, [2017] | Series: Dogs ; set 13 | Includes index.
Identifiers: LCCN 2016007743 (print) | LCCN 2016016985 (ebook) | ISBN 9781680781755 (print) | ISBN 9781680775600 (ebook)
Subjects: LCSH: Hounds--Juvenile literature. | Dog breeds--Juvenile literature.
Classification: LCC SF429.H6 P65 2016 (print) | LCC SF429.H6 (ebook) | DDC 636.753/6--dc23
LC record available at https://lccn.loc.gov/2016007743

Contents

The Dog Family

Dogs are one of the most popular pets in the world. There are more than 70 million pet dogs in the United States alone! Dog and human relationships extend back thousands of years. The first **domesticated** dogs helped humans hunt and warned them of danger. They also helped them herd livestock.

There are more than 400 dog **breeds** worldwide. They come in many different shapes, sizes, and colors. But they all belong to the family **Canidae**. Wolves, coyotes, and foxes belong to this family too. In fact, scientists believe dogs descended from the gray wolf.

Dogs today are much different from their wild ancestors. Many serve as companions. Others have special jobs such as guarding or hunting. The bluetick coonhound is one of the top hunting dogs. It also loves people and makes a smart, energetic pet.

The bluetick coonhound inherited its hunting skills from the gray wolf.

Bluetick Coonhounds

Bluetick coonhounds were specially **bred** to hunt. Breeders traveled to the Ozark Mountains and Louisiana bayous to develop expert tracking hounds. They bred French staghounds with American English foxhounds. This created the American English coonhound. The English coonhound was fast and had an excellent sense of smell.

In 1945, one group broke away from the American English coonhound breeders. They developed a slower, **cold-nosed** hound. They named it the bluetick coonhound after the markings on its fur. This large hound had a powerful nose and amazing **endurance**. It was very popular among hunters.

The **United Kennel Club (UKC)** recognized the bluetick coonhound in 1946. The **American Kennel Club (AKC)** didn't recognize the **breed** until 2009.

What They're Like

The bluetick coonhound is a big bundle of energy. It is also very intelligent. Although the bluetick can be stubborn, it is also eager to please. Praise and food rewards can be used to train this **breed**.

This friendly hound loves people and grows very attached to its owners. It likes to be right by your side. It's also great with children, which makes it a wonderful family pet. But it was bred to be a tracking dog. So, while the bluetick may enjoy napping, it is also quick to chase a scent.

The bluetick coonhound was also bred to be noisy. Each one has a special **bawl** used to alert hunters of a trail. Even when it's not hunting, this dog has a lot to say. This breed is not recommended for apartments!

A bluetick coonhound named Smokey leads the University of Tennessee football team onto the field before games.

Coat and Color

The bluetick coat is short, glossy, and very colorful. Most blueticks have black spots on their backs, ears, and sides. Some have a white stripe along their snouts. But every bluetick has thick, dark-blue **ticked** fur on its body. This freckled blue-and-white pattern gave the bluetick its name.

This **breed** can have red ticking on its chest, feet, and lower legs. It can also have tan markings on its cheeks and forehead. This dog's smooth coat doesn't **shed** much and requires little grooming.

Blueticks give off a strong, musty scent. This is common for certain hound breeds. Even if you bathe a bluetick, its scent won't disappear completely. Yet many people grow to love this "houndy" smell!

The bluetick is known for its smooth, spotted coat.

Size

While the bluetick loves to snuggle, it's not exactly a lapdog. This medium-sized **breed** has a compact, muscular build. Females generally weigh 45 to 65 pounds (20 to 29 kg). Males are often larger and weigh 55 to 80 pounds (25 to 36 kg).

Adult females stand 21 to 25 inches (53 to 64 cm) tall. Males measure 22 to 27 inches (56 to 69 cm) in height.

The bluetick has big paws and powerful legs. It can jump very high. This mischief-maker is even known to steal food from countertops!

The bluetick has a broad, **domed** head with low, floppy ears. Its **muzzle** is long and square. Its big, dark brown eyes give its face a pleading look. But its large nose is the star of the show. The wide nostrils are perfect for sniffing out trails.

A strong build helps
the bluetick hunt for
raccoons in the forest.

Care

With proper care, the bluetick is usually quite healthy. But it is important to visit a veterinarian for regular checkups. The vet can give your dog **vaccines** and **spay** or **neuter** it. The vet will also check for common problems such as **hip dysplasia**.

Basic grooming will also keep your bluetick feeling great. Check and clean its ears weekly to prevent infection. Brush its coat and trim its nails regularly. You can even brush your dog's teeth with special toothpaste! This will prevent tooth decay and gum disease.

The energetic bluetick needs plenty of exercise. It will grow bored and mischievous without it. Daily walks and playtime can help keep your bluetick out of trouble!

Occasional brushing will keep your bluetick's coat clean and glossy.

Feeding

The bluetick needs quality fuel to stay active! Its diet will depend on its age, size, and lifestyle. There are many different dry, wet, and semi-moist foods available. Your vet can help you determine which food is right for your dog. It should be rich in protein and healthy fats.

Your bluetick puppy should eat about three meals a day. It should eat the same food its **breeder** gave it. Adult blueticks should eat one to two meals a day. Dogs of every age should always have fresh water available. Make any food changes gradually to help your dog adjust.

Be careful not to overfeed your bluetick. Treats should be given in moderation, and avoid feeding your dog table scraps. **Obesity** causes major health problems for dogs. This can include joint problems and heart disease. A proper diet will give your bluetick a longer, happier life!

Those sad hound eyes are great at begging. But go easy on the treats!

Things They Need

The bluetick needs patient training and praise from a young age. Your bluetick will need a leash, collar, and identification tags for its daily walks. A fenced-in yard is also recommended. The fence will prevent your hound from chasing after scent trails!

Like all dogs, your bluetick will appreciate a comfortable bed. A roomy crate will prevent accidents while you are away. It will also give your bluetick a nice place to rest. An assortment of safe toys will help entertain your pup.

Most importantly, the bluetick needs lots of love and attention. Spend time with your dog. Play with it.

Relax together. Whatever the activity, your hound will want to join you!

A dog bed will do just fine.
But any bluetick will appreciate
a spot on the couch!

Puppies

A bluetick coonhound **pregnancy** lasts about 63 days. The mother then gives birth to a **litter** of puppies. There are usually seven to eight pups in each litter.

The puppies are born deaf and blind. Their ears and eyes start working after two weeks. At six weeks old, the puppies are ready for their first **vaccinations**.

When you are ready for your own bluetick, do your research! Choose a qualified **breeder** or shelter. Spend time with the puppies before choosing one. Make sure it is healthy and well treated. Your bluetick can come home when it is eight weeks old.

Begin training your puppy right away. Gradually introduce it to new people and places. A healthy bluetick will be an enthusiastic family member for 12 to 14 years.

Talkative bluetick pups will grow
to be loyal, loving companions.

Glossary

American Kennel Club (AKC) - an organization that studies and promotes interest in purebred dogs.

bawl - a loud, long cry that certain hounds make.

breed - a group of animals sharing the same ancestors and appearance. A breeder is a person who raises animals. Raising animals is often called breeding them.

Canidae (KAN-uh-dee) - the scientific Latin name for the dog family. Members of this family are called canids. They include wolves, jackals, foxes, coyotes, and domestic dogs.

cold-nosed - able to pick up the scent of trails that are not as fresh, often called "cold trails."

domed - having a rounded top.

domesticated - adapted to life with humans.

endurance - the ability to sustain a long, stressful effort or activity.

hip dysplasia (HIHP dihs-PLAY-zhuh) - unusual formation of the hip joint.

litter - all of the puppies born at one time to a mother dog.

muzzle - an animal's nose and jaws.

neuter (NOO-tuhr) - to remove a male animal's reproductive glands.

obesity - the condition of having too much body fat.

pregnancy - having one or more babies growing within the body.

shed - to cast off hair, feathers, skin, or other coverings or parts by a natural process.

spay - to remove a female animal's reproductive organs.

ticked - having hair banded with two or more colors.

United Kennel Club (UKC) - an organization that studies and promotes interest in purebred dogs.

vaccine (vak-SEEN) - a shot given to prevent illness or disease. The act of giving someone a vaccine is a vaccination.

Websites

To learn more about Dogs, visit **booklinks.abdopublishing.com**. These links are routinely monitored and updated to provide the most current information available.

Index